Contents

Immigration Island	4
The Journey Begins	10
Island of Hope and Tears	18
Starting New Lives	32
Learning More	46
Glossary	47
Index	48

Immigration Island

Sailing to America

"Riding on a big boat across the Atlantic Ocean may sound like fun, but it wasn't. The two-week trip was miserable! Our beds were ... way down in the bottom of the boat. It was lined with bunks, one on top of the other. It was uncomfortable and crowded. I went up on deck all the time, just to have space to move around." This is how Seymour Rechtzeit, a Jewish **immigrant** from Poland, remembered his journey to Ellis Island.

Millions of Immigrants

During the late 1800s and early 1900s, millions of immigrants journeyed across the Atlantic Ocean or the Pacific Ocean by steamship. Men, women, and children from Europe, Asia, and other parts of the world dreamed of living in North America. From 1892–1954, more than 12 million immigrants arrived in the United States and their first stop on American soil was the Ellis Island Immigration Station in New York City.

▼ *The journey to America was long and hard, but millions of immigrants made the trip, hoping it would bring them a better life.*

"On the boat ... they piled us up eight or ten people in one cabin, and the food was the worst that it could be."

Sam Auspitz, immigrated from Czechoslovakia in 1920

immigrant: someone who comes to live in a new country

The Island

Ellis Island is an island in New York Harbor. It lies about one milc (1.6 kilometers) southwest of Manhattan Island. The site was chosen as an immigration station because it was big enough to contain the large crowds of immigrants that were expected to arrive each day. The Ellis Island Immigration Station officially opened on January 1, 1892.

Landing in America

Immigrants that arrived at Ellis Island came from many different countries in Europe and Asia. The majority came from Italy, Russia, Poland, Spain, and Greece. They saw America as a land of opportunity. They helped America's population grow, worked hard at different jobs, and brought new languages and cultures to America.

Since 1820, more than 75 million immigrants came to live in the United States. They came from Europe, Central and South America, Asia, Africa, and other parts of the world.

◀ *This photo shows the Ellis Island Immigration Station as it looks now. Almost half of America's citizens have* ***ancestors*** *who came through Ellis Island.*

ancestors: members of someone's family from the past

Starvation and War

During the 1800s, many people living in Europe, Asia, and other continents were very poor and had difficult lives. For example, between 1846 and 1851, about one million people in Ireland died in a **famine** known as the Great Famine. In other parts of Europe, millions of other people were being killed in violent wars and for religious and political reasons.

▶ *This magazine illustration from 1880 shows an Irish woman asking an American ship for help. The message on the rock below her says "We are starving."*

The journey to America was long, but steamships made the journey faster. Steamships were big ocean liners with engines that ran on steam. At first, they transported mainly cargo, but they soon started carrying passengers, too. Tickets for steamships were also less expensive than the tickets for sailing ships. For these reasons, many more people decided to make the trip to America.

▲ *Many immigrants traveled on steamships. This picture shows the SS* Egypt *and SS* Spain, *which sailed between New York and Liverpool, England.*

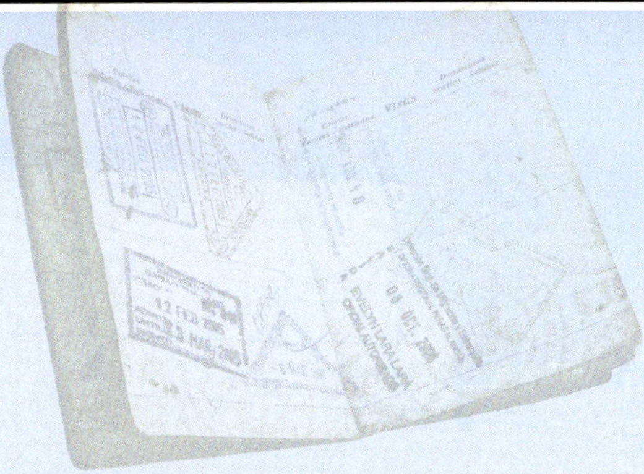

Dream of a New Life

In America, people had more opportunities and rights. There were more jobs, and life was easier and safer. During this time, there were very few rules to stop people immigrating and it was easy to find work. Immigrants who were already in America sent letters to their relatives and friends, encouraging them to come to America.

famine: an extreme shortage of food

The Journey Begins

Saying Goodbye

Most immigrants arrived in North America by sea. To board a steamship, immigrants first had to make their way to the closest **seaport** in their home country. This trip was often long and exhausting. Because people had to carry their own belongings, they brought few possessions with them. They said good-bye to relatives, friends, and their ways of life.

▲ *These Greek immigrants are traveling by boat to the steamship that will carry them to America.*

All Aboard!

Once they reached seaports, they boarded steamships. Immigrants from Asia traveled across the Pacific Ocean. Many entered the United States through Angel Island in San Francisco, California. Immigrants moving from Europe to the United States usually entered through Ellis Island. Those moving to Canada entered the country at Grosse Isle, Quebec, or at Pier 21 in Halifax, Nova Scotia.

▶ *This map shows the main ports through which immigrants entered North America.*

The Angel Island Immigration Station opened in 1910 in an area that became known as China Cove. Immigrants from more than 80 different countries came through there, but most were Chinese.

seaports: ports or harbors that can be used by seagoing ships

Different Classes

The wealthiest passengers got to stay on the top levels of the ship. They stayed in private **staterooms** and cabins. Third-class passengers stayed in steerage, which was the lowest level of the ship usually used to hold cargo. Steerage was divided into large rooms, and hundreds of people slept together stacked in bunks.

▲ *The upper levels of ships were cleaner and more comfortable than the lower levels.*

Crowded Ships

Steamship companies competed for passengers and packed up to 3,000 people onto each ship. Living side-by-side with so many people who spoke different languages and practiced different religions was difficult. Family members and friends tried to stay together on the journey, which usually took between one and two weeks from Europe.

◀ *This Italian family traveled to Ellis Island in about 1905.*

"We spent eleven days on board the ship. The first four days we were deathly sick, seasick, because we were down in [steerage]. The cheapest possible ticket ... I was so sick, and I wanted to die. I was seven years old."

Rota Fichbach, immigrated from Germany in 1926

staterooms: private rooms on a ship

Hard Journey

The journey across the Atlantic Ocean was terrible. Steamships were crowded and dirty, especially in steerage. Steerage was jam-packed, filthy, and had hardly any fresh air. There were no windows and no room to move around. There were no proper toilets. Two or three of every five steerage passengers suffered from seasickness.

▲ *Many passengers became tired and weary during the long trip across the Atlantic Ocean.*

Spreading Sickness

Diseases and other illnesses spread quickly on the ships because they were so crowded and dirty. Many people got trachoma, a contagious eye disease that caused blindness. Other people got sick with typhoid, an infection caused by bacteria in **contaminated** food or water. Immigrants who were sick or weak would be held back at the immigration station.

> **"[The trip from Europe] was rough. The food was bad. You couldn't even eat at a table. We used to eat like beggars there, we ate sitting on the floor ..."**
>
> Tessie Croce, immigrated from Italy in 1912, age 15

contaminated: not pure and so unsafe to eat or drink

Excited and Anxious

Despite the long, hard journey, immigrants were excited to arrive in America. They were anxious to begin their new lives. Immigrants with family and friends already in America were excited to be reunited. To these men, women, and children, America meant a fresh start. It was a place where hopes and dreams could come true.

▼ *The Statue of Liberty, also known as Lady Liberty, is a famous symbol of freedom. For the people sailing into New York Harbor, it represented the dream of a new life in America.*

"Give me your tired, your poor, Your huddled masses yearning to breathe free ... "

From a plaque on the Statue of Liberty

Statue and Symbol

As the ships arrived in New York Harbor, immigrants caught sight of the Statue of **Liberty**. This famous statue stands on its own island in the harbor. People in steerage scrambled to the upper decks to catch a glimpse of the statue. They sometimes cheered or cried with joy as their ships passed by it.

▼ *The Statue of Liberty is just over 305 feet (93 meters) tall from the base to the torch.*

liberty: freedom and independence

Inspecting Immigrants

When ships arrived in New York Harbor, immigrants had to go through an inspection process, which included medical and **legal** inspections. Doctors checked the first- and second-class passengers aboard their ships. The government believed that people who could afford to buy first- or second-class tickets were less likely to have diseases or rely on the government for help with living expenses.

Free to Enter

After being processed, those who were healthy could get off the ship in New York City. They passed through customs at the piers and were free to enter the United States. However, first- and second-class passengers who were sick or had legal problems were sent to Ellis Island for further inspection.

When the Ellis Island Immigration Station officially opened in January of 1892, 15-year-old Annie Moore became the first immigrant to pass through its doors. She and her two brothers came from Ireland and were processed on Annie's birthday.

◀ *This statue shows Annie Moore and her two brothers. The children came to America to be reunited with their parents who were already in New York.*

legal: to do with the law

▼ *These immigrants are lined up to have their legal documents examined and signed by immigration officers.*

Waiting for Processing

Other passengers, including third-class passengers, did not have it as easy. About three-quarters of each ship's passengers were taken to Ellis Island for immigration processing and most were from third class. During the peak immigration years, Ellis Island was so overcrowded that some immigrants had to wait several days on their ships before smaller ferryboats could transfer them to Ellis Island.

"... there was this slight feeling among many of us that, 'Isn't it strange that here we are coming to a country where there is complete equality, but not quite so for the newly arrived immigrants.'"

Hans Bergner, arrived at Ellis Island in 1924

Fear and Confusion

Many third-class passengers were sick and exhausted. Some had diseases. Most could not speak English. When they were finally allowed onto Ellis Island, these immigrants were scared and confused about why they were there and where they were going. They were terrified of being turned away and sent back to the countries from which they fled.

equality: being equal, having the same rights and freedom

▶ *Immigrants carried their belongings up the stairs to the Registry Room.*

Climb to the Top

Officers shouted and tried to direct the immigrants as they struggled off the ships. The **commotion** only added to the immigrants' confusion. The immigrants were eventually directed to a flight of winding stairs that led to the Registry Room.

Being Watched

As the immigrants climbed the stairs, doctors looked for any signs of sickness or physical disabilities. They looked for people who were coughing, having trouble breathing or walking, or who looked weak. Sick or weak immigrants would be forced to return to their home countries or required to stay in hospitals on Ellis Island, often without their relatives.

"When the doctor examined me, he discovered I had a cold. He said I could not go with my father, though I cried and begged. I was terrified to be all alone in this strange place."

Seymour Rechtzeit, a Jewish immigrant from Poland

▲ *The arched windows at Ellis Island gave immigrants a tantalizing view of what they hoped would be their new home. They were afraid of being detained or sent back to their home countries.*

commotion: noisy excitement and confusion

Six Seconds

Processing in the Registry Room was designed to move people quickly and efficiently. First, doctors performed what came to be known as a "six-second physical" to identify signs of sickness or diseases that could be spread. They also looked for any sign of physical problems. The people doctors suspected were sick were marked with chalk.

▼ *The Registry Room measured 200 feet (61 meters) long and 102 feet (31 meters) wide.*

Chalked Up

The chalk marks were coded for different health issues. For example, the letter B indicated a bad back, the letter C indicated **conjunctivitis**, the letter E indicated bad eyes, the letter H indicated a heart condition, and a circled letter X indicated a mental health problem. Immigrants who were marked with chalk were held back for further inspection.

The Registry Room, also called the Great Hall, could hold about 5,000 people. To keep everyone in order, immigrants were made to form lines between long rails and wait their turn for inspection.

conjunctivitis: an eye condition, also known as pink eye

Trachoma Check

A common health concern in the early 1900s was an eye disease called trachoma. It led to more people being held back and **deported** than any other sickness during that time. Checking for trachoma was painful and many immigrants dreaded this part of the medical exam, especially children.

▶ *This photo shows doctors checking immigrants for trachoma.*

Before 1945, women could not immigrate alone to the United States. Back then, most women did not have paying jobs. Immigration officials worried that a woman on her own would become a burden on her new country.

Flipping Out

To check for trachoma, doctors would flip up each eyelid with a buttonhook or hairpin. They were looking for the roughening of the inner surface of the eyelids. Doctors tried to work quickly, but the procedure was uncomfortable. Immigrants with trachoma were not allowed into America. They were often sent back to their home countries.

deported: forced to leave a country

Answering Questions

After passing the medical examinations, immigrants waited in the Great Hall for their legal inspections. The legal inspection included a list of questions, including name, age, occupation, nationality, and final destination. The answers were cross-checked with the information on the ships' **manifests**, which were made before the ships left for America.

"The work on the island was difficult and strenuous ... Immigrants were pouring in at the average rate of 5,000 a day and it was a constant grind from the moment we got into our uniforms early in the morning until the last minute before we left ..."

Fiorello LaGuardia, future mayor of New York, worked as an interpreter at Ellis Island

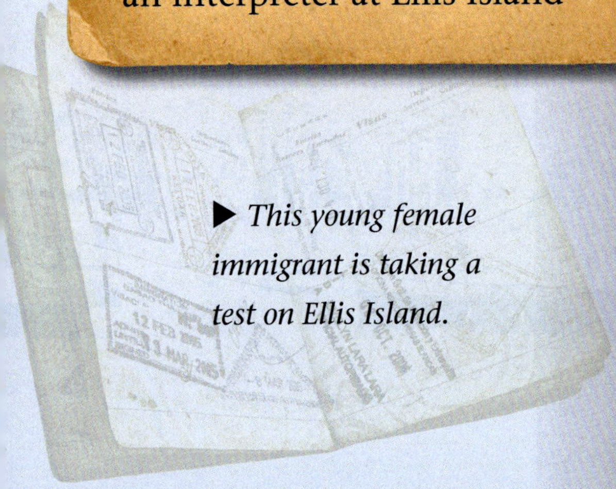

▶ *This young female immigrant is taking a test on Ellis Island.*

Reading and Writing

Interpreters helped the immigrants communicate their answers, but there was much confusion and misunderstanding between the inspectors and the immigrants. Starting in 1917, immigrants also had to pass reading and writing tests. Immigrants over the age of 16 who could not read between 30 and 40 test words in their language were not allowed into the United States. They were sent back to their home countries.

manifests: lists of passengers

Island of Hope

Most of the immigrants passed through the legal and medical inspections with little trouble. Inspections usually lasted about three to five hours and then the immigrants were free to begin their new lives in America. They were reunited with relatives and friends and could focus on realizing their hopes and dreams in their new country.

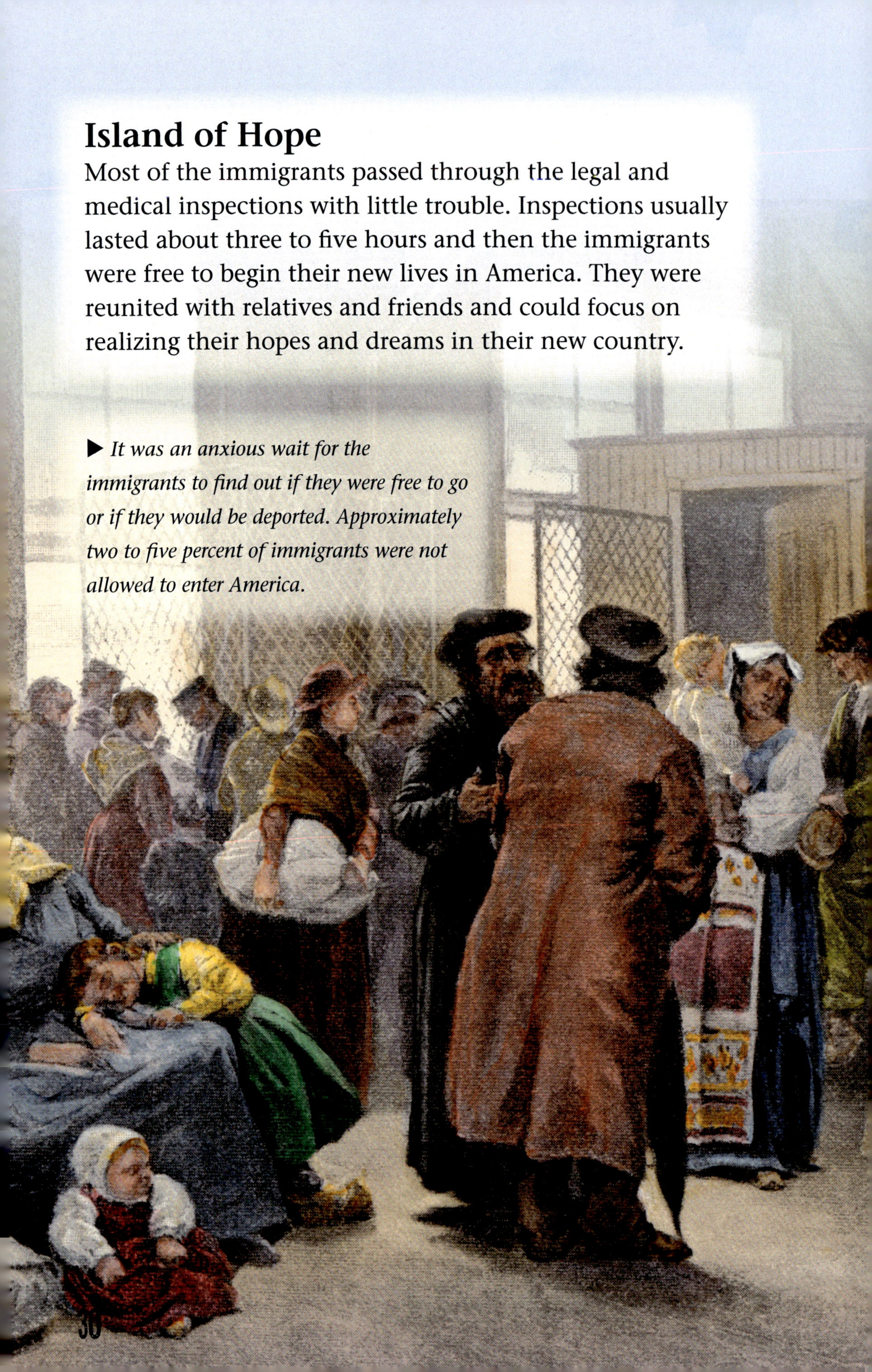

▶ *It was an anxious wait for the immigrants to find out if they were free to go or if they would be deported. Approximately two to five percent of immigrants were not allowed to enter America.*

Island of Tears

For some immigrants, Ellis Island was an island of tears. They could be turned away if they were diagnosed with a dangerous disease or if a legal inspector believed they were likely to work illegally or rely on the government for help. These immigrants were put into **quarantine** or sent back to their home countries.

Outside of the Registry Room, there was a wooden column where friends and relatives greeted each other, usually with tears, hugs, and kisses. For this reason, the wooden column was nicknamed The Kissing Post.

quarantine: a place where sick people are kept apart from others

Starting New Lives

Adjusting to America

Although immigrant **aid** societies helped some immigrants to find their relatives and get jobs and homes, life was hard for the new immigrants. Many did not speak English, most were very poor, and everyone was unfamiliar with the new customs and practices in America.

▼ *This picture shows the Chinese residents of San Francisco celebrating New Year in 1871.*

Immigrant Communities

Over time, immigrants formed tight-knit communities. Immigrants from the same countries lived in the same neighborhoods or on the same blocks. For example, certain areas in cities became known as Little Italy and Chinatown. This sense of community was a comfort, but immigrants struggled to make ends meet. Often, immigrants could only find backbreaking work in iron, steel, mining, and lumber industries.

> **"I came to America because I heard the streets were paved with gold. When I got here, I found out three things: First, the streets weren't paved with gold; second, they weren't paved at all: and third, I was expected to pave them."**
>
> Italian immigrant

aid: help

Racism in America

Immigrants also faced **racism** in America. Some Americans felt that the new immigrants were taking jobs away from people who had been born in the United States. These people formed nativist groups. Nativists were American-born citizens who had an extreme dislike for immigrants. They wanted to stop immigrants from coming to the United States.

"Crazy old buildings, crowded rear tenements in filthy yards, dark, damp basements, leaking garrets, shops, outhouses, and stables converted into dwellings, though scarcely fit to shelter brutes, are habitations of thousands of our fellow-beings in this wealthy, Christian city."

Jacob Riis, immigrated from Denmark in 1870

Other Hardships

Immigrants often had to take whatever work was offered, no matter how little the pay or unsafe the working conditions. They faced other hardships, too. Many lived in overcrowded tenement buildings, which were old, rundown buildings divided into apartments. Some had no indoor toilets. Many had no electricity, so immigrants used kerosene or oil lamps. Before housing and workplace safety laws were put in place, many newcomers died of disease or in fires.

◀ *This picture shows an alley known as "Bandit's Roost" in Little Italy, New York City, in the 1890s. The area was well known for being dangerous and run-down.*

racism: hatred or dislike based on someone's race

Ellis Island of the West

Immigrants arriving at Angel Island, in San Francisco, California, faced similar struggles. Angel Island opened in 1910 and was often called the "Ellis Island of the West." Approximately one million immigrants went through the island from 1910 to 1940.

> **"Many Chinese were detained in Angel Island anywhere from two weeks to several months ... A few people were detained up to two years!"**
>
> Seven-year-old Li Keng Wong, immigrated from China to California in 1933

▲ *These Chinese boys are waiting for medical examinations on Angel Island.*

Chinese Immigrants

Many of these immigrants were from China. They believed that there were more opportunities and better living conditions in America. Many Americans disliked all the Chinese immigrants, however. The immigrants were willing to work longer hours for less money. Americans believed that the Chinese immigrants were taking their jobs.

▼ *This cartoon from 1882 shows San Franciscans throwing stones at recently arrived Chinese immigrants.*

detained: made to stay somewhere

Reasons to Immigrate

Immigrants were also arriving in parts of Canada. Many came to Canada to escape floods and **droughts**, wars, and religious or political problems in their countries. There were new settlements and industries, such as mining and lumber, throughout Canada. There was also a growing railway network, known today as the Canadian Pacific Railway.

Coming to Canada

During the early to mid-19th century, immigrants were coming to Canada from Ireland, England, Scotland, France, Belgium, and many other parts of Europe. Immigrants also came from China, Japan, and other Asian countries. Over the past 100 years, more than 13 million immigrants have arrived in Canada from all over the world.

During the late 1800s, some native-born Americans and Canadians began having difficulty finding jobs and were earning less money because there were so many Chinese workers. In 1882, the United States government passed the Chinese Exclusion Act, which restricted Chinese immigration for ten years. In 1885, the Canadian government passed the Chinese Immigration Act, which forced each Chinese immigrant to pay a $50 tax to enter Canada.

◀ *Unable to get a job in Scotland, these Scots left for Canada in 1925. Their sign explains that they would rather be employed in Canada than get unemployment payments (the dole) in their homeland.*

droughts: long periods of time without rain

▲ *Grosse Isle is now also known as the Irish Memorial National Historic Site.*

Grosse Isle

Many Irish immigrants came to Canada through Grosse Isle, Quebec, to escape the Great Famine in Ireland. Grosse Isle is in the Gulf of St. Lawrence in Quebec, Canada. It was a quarantine station for the Port of Quebec, which was the main arrival site for immigrants coming into Canada.

◀ *Approximately 500,000 Irish immigrants passed through Grosse Isle between 1832 and 1932.*

Pier 21

Between 1928 and 1971, one million immigrants and **refugees** arrived at the port called Pier 21 in Halifax, Nova Scotia, Canada. They came to Canada from Europe and other parts of the world. Pier 21 was also a departure point for nearly 500,000 Canadian troops during World War II. In 1997, it became a National Historic Site of Canada and officially became a National Museum of Canada in 2011.

In 1847, an epidemic of typhoid claimed the lives of over 5,000 immigrants. Most of the immigrants were Irish and were buried at Grosse Isle. Another 5,000 immigrants died at sea and thousands more died in cities elsewhere in Canada.

refugees: people who flee for safety to foreign countries

◀ *This photo, taken in the 1980s, shows how the hospital building on Ellis Island looked after 30 years of neglect.*

Immigration Begins to Decline

Immigration at Ellis Island began to decline shortly after World War I. Americans were becoming more and more resentful of immigrants. In 1924, the government stepped in and Congress passed the National Origins Act, which placed restrictions and **quotas** on who could enter America. Ellis Island was officially closed on November 12, 1954.

Shaping the Future

The immigrants who arrived at Ellis Island and other places in North America helped shape the future of both America and Canada. They increased the population and workforce. They helped industries and cities to grow. Many immigrants went on to make important contributions to science, entertainment, art, language, and various industries.

"My family's beginning in this country is but one of thousands tied to Ellis Island. To me, the place holds as much history and more personal stories than any spot in America—twelve million, to be exact."

Lee Iacocca, former Chairman of Chrysler Corporation and famous Italian-American businessman

◀ *For the vast majority of immigrants, Ellis Island was the start of a new life and new opportunities.*

quotas: fixed amounts

Ellis Island Today

Today, Ellis Island is a symbol for the American immigrant experience and for immigration throughout North America. For most immigrants, Ellis Island was the first stop on the way to freedom, new opportunities, and better lives. Today, immigration to America is high once again. Immigrants from Asia, Latin America, and Africa arrive every year. America is now a **multicultural** society.

Immigration Museum

In 1982, the Statue of Liberty-Ellis Island Foundation was established. The foundation is dedicated to restoration, preservation, and education at Ellis Island and the Statue of Liberty. In 1990, after years of restoration, the foundation opened the Ellis Island Immigration Museum. Rooms have been carefully restored to look as they did during the height of immigration processing.

◀ *Over 12 million immigrants came through Ellis Island. The Ellis Island Immigration Museum tells some of their stories.*

"I remember my grandfather always telling me how he knew he could be rich in America because he saw riches in the architecture of Ellis Island. He felt that if they let the poor in such a gorgeous hall then life in this country was just."

Rosanne Welch, granddaughter of Giuseppe Italiano, an Italian immigrant in 1904

multicultural: relating to different cultures

Learning More

Books

Ellis Island (True Books) by Elaine Landau Sherman (Childrens Press, 2008)

Ellis Island (Cornerstones of Freedom) by Melissa McDaniel (Childrens Press, 2011)

At Ellis Island: A History in Many Voices by Louise Peacock and Walter Lyon Krudop (Atheneum Books for Young Readers, 2007)

Hope and Tears: Ellis Island Voices by Gwenyth Swain (Calkind Creek, 2012)

Websites

Ellis Island National Monument
http://www.nps.gov/elis/index.htm

The Statue of Liberty-Ellis Island Foundation
http://www.ellisisland.org/

Ellis Island – History, Articles, Video, Pictures, and Facts
http://www.history.com/topics/ellis-island

Save Ellis Island
http://saveellisisland.org/

Glossary

aid Help

ancestors Members of someone's family from the past

commotion Noisy excitement and confusion

conjunctivitis An eye condition, also known as pink eye

contaminated Not pure and so unsafe to eat or drink

deported Forced to leave a country

detained Made to stay somewhere

droughts Long periods of time without rain

equality Being equal, having the same rights and freedom

famine An extreme shortage of food

immigrant Someone who comes to live in a new country

legal To do with the law

liberty Freedom and independence

manifests Lists of passengers

multicultural Relating to different cultures

quarantine A place where sick people are kept apart from others

quotas Fixed amounts

racism Hatred or dislike based on someone's race

refugees People who flee for safety to foreign countries

seaports Ports or harbors that can be used by seagoing ships

staterooms Private rooms on a ship

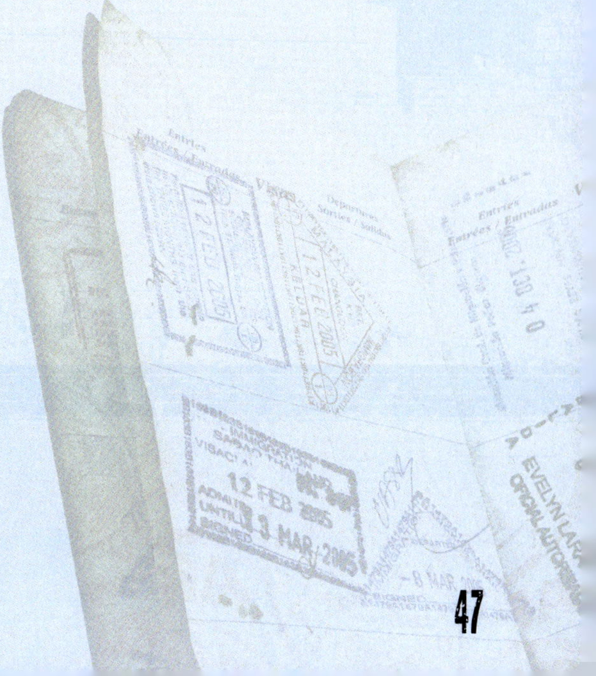

Index

Entries in **bold** refer to pictures

Africa 7, 44
Angel Island 11, 36
Asia 5, 7, 8, 11, 39, 44
Atlantic Ocean 4, 5, 14

Canada 11, 38, 39, 40, 41, 43
Central America 7
children 5, 16, **18–19**, 26
Chinatown 33
Chinese Exclusion Act 39
Chinese immigrants 11, 36, **36**, **36–37**, 37, 39
Chinese Immigration Act 39
Czechoslovakian immigrants 5

diseases 15, 18, 21, 24, 26, 31, 35

Europe 5, 7, 8, 11, 13, 15, 39, 41

famine 8, 40

Greek immigrants **10**
Grosse Isle 11, 40, **40–41**, 41

Halifax 11, 41
hospitals 23, **42**

industries 33, 38, 43
inspections 18, 19, 25, 28, 30
Ireland 8, 19, 39, 40
Irish immigrants 41
Italian immigrants **13**, 33

Jewish immigrants 4, 23
jobs 7, 9, 32, 34, 37, 39

Latin America 44
Little Italy 33, **34–35**

Moore, Annie **18–19**, 19
museums 41, **44–45**, 45

National Historic Sites **40–41**, 41
National Origins Act 42

Pacific Ocean 5, 11
passengers 8, 12, 14, **14–15**, 18, 19, 20, 21
Pier 21 11, 41
ports **11**, 30

racism 34
Registry Room 22, **24–25**, 25, 31

San Francisco 11, 30, **32–33**, 36
Scottish immigrants **38–39**
seaports 10, 11
seasickness 13, 14
South America 7
Statue of Liberty 16, **16**, 17, **17**, 45
steamships 5, 8, **9**, 10, 11, 12, 13, 14
steerage 12, 13, 14, 17

trachoma 15, 26, 27
typhoid 15, 41

World War I 42
World War II 26, 41

ELLIS ISLAND

Molly Aloian

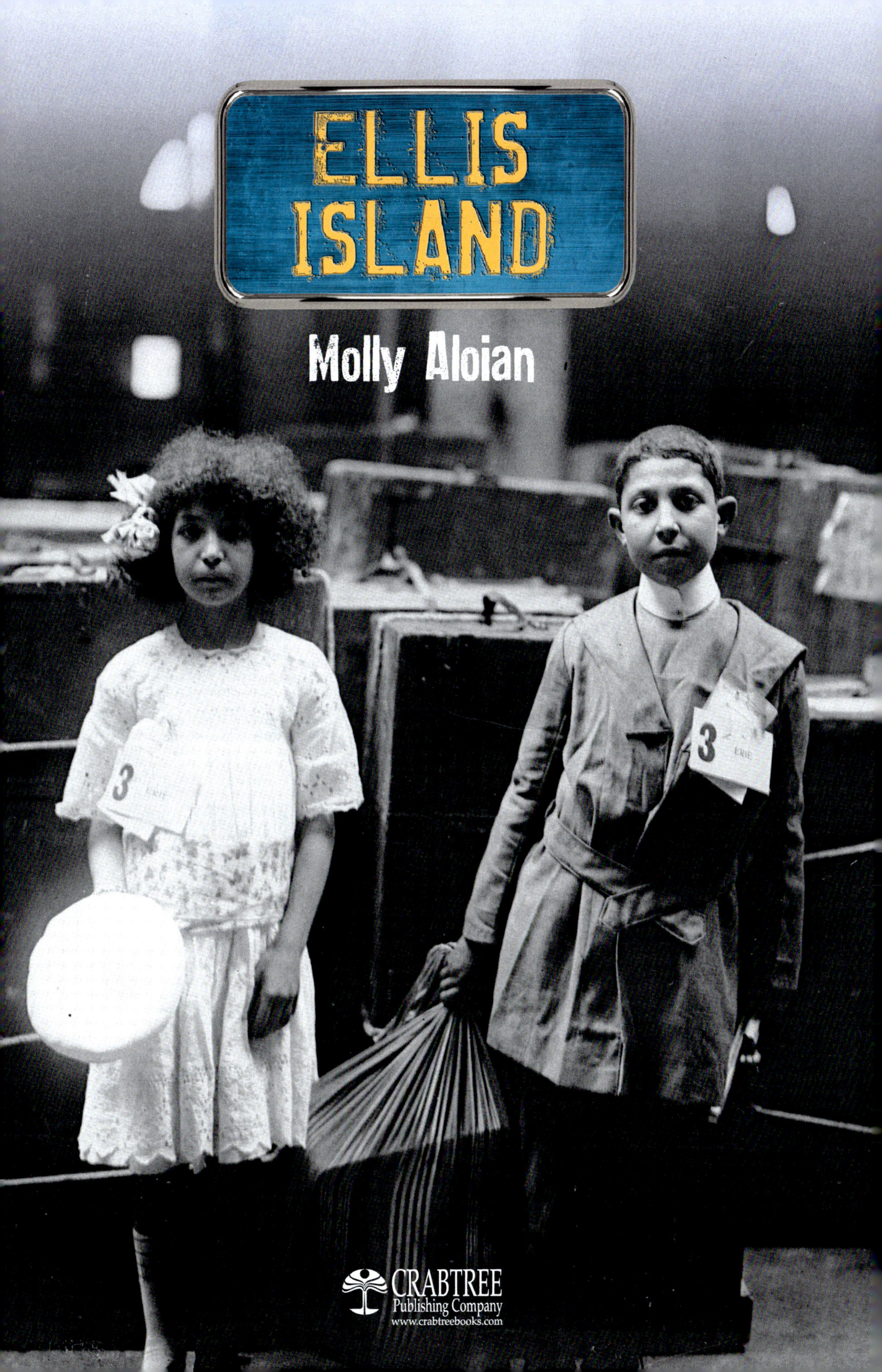

CRABTREE
Publishing Company
www.crabtreebooks.com

Crabtree Publishing Company
www.crabtreebooks.com

Author: Molly Aloian
Publishing plan research and development: Reagan Miller
Editors: Rachel Minay, Kathy Middleton
Proofreader: Adrianna Morganelli
Photo researchers: Molly Aloian, Rachel Minay
Book design: Tim Mayer
Cover design: Ken Wright
Production coordinator and prepress tecnician: Ken Wright
Print coordinator: Margaret Amy Salter

Produced for Crabtree Publishing Company by White-Thomson Publishing

Photographs:
Alamy: Judy Waytiuk: p. 40; North Wind Picture Archives: pp. 30–31; Bridgeman Art Library: Bridgeman Universal History Archive/UIG: pp. 4–5; Private Collection/ Peter Newark American Pictures: p. 16; Corbis: pp. 32–33; Bettmann: pp. 20–21, 34–35; Hulton-Deutsch Collection: pp. 38–39; Lewis Wickes Hine/Brooklyn Museum: p. 22; Underwood & Underwood: pp. 24–25; Getty: pp. 12, 28–29; Library of Congress: pp. 1, 3, 6–7, 8, 9, 10, 42, 44–45, 46; Mary Evans Picture Library: pp. 36–37; Shutterstock: front and back cover; Shutterstock: Joy Strotz: p. 23; Luis Santos: pp. 18–19; meunierd: pp. 40–41; Miroslav Halama: p. 17; Vlad G: p. 43; Topfoto: The Granger Collection: pp. 13, 14–15, 26–27, 36; White-Thomson Publishing/Stefan Chabluk: p. 11.

Library and Archives Canada Cataloguing in Publication

Aloian, Molly, author
Ellis Island / Molly Aloian.

(Crabtree chrome)
Includes index.
Issued also in electronic formats.
ISBN 978-0-7787-1168-1 (bound).--ISBN 978-0-7787-1176-6 (pbk.).--
ISBN 978-1-4271-8929-5 (pdf).--ISBN 978-1-4271-8921-9 (html)

1. Ellis Island Immigration Station (N.Y. and N.J.)--History--Juvenile literature. 2. Ellis Island (N.J. and N.Y.)--History--Juvenile literature. 3. Immigrants--United States--History--Juvenile literature. 4. United States--Emigration and immigration--History--Juvenile literature. I. Title. II. Series: Crabtree chrome

JV6484.A56 2014 j304.8'73 C2013-907561-5
C2013-907562-3

Library of Congress Cataloging-in-Publication Data

Aloian, Molly.
Ellis Island / Molly Aloian.
pages cm. -- (Crabtree chrome)
Includes index.
ISBN 978-0-7787-1168-1 (reinforced library binding) -- ISBN 978-0-7787-1176-6 (pbk.) -- ISBN 978-1-4271-8929-5 (electronic pdf) -- ISBN 978-1-4271-8921-9 (electronic html)
1. Ellis Island Immigration Station (N.Y. and N.J.)--Juvenile literature. 2. United States--Emigration and immigration--History--Juvenile literature. I. Title.

JV6484.A46 2014
304.8'73--dc23

2013043383

Crabtree Publishing Company
www.crabtreebooks.com 1-800-387-7650

Printed in Canada/122022/CPC20221201

Published in Canada
Crabtree Publishing
616 Welland Ave.
St. Catharines, ON
L2M 5V6

Published in the United States
Crabtree Publishing
347 Fifth Ave
Suite 1402-145
New York, NY 10016

Published in the United Kingdom
Crabtree Publishing
Maritime House
Basin Road North, Hove
BN41 1WR

Published in Australia
Crabtree Publishing
Unit 3-5
Currumbin Court
Capalaba QLD 4157